A Day in the Life: Sea Animals

Jellyfish

Louise Spilsbury

Heinemann Library
Chicago, Illinois

H www.heinemannraintree.com
Visit our website to find out
more information about
Heinemann-Raintree books.

To order:
☏ Phone 888-454-2279
🖳 Visit www.heinemannraintree.com
   to browse our catalog and order online.

Edited by Sian Smith, Nancy Dickmann,
   and Rebecca Rissman
Designed by Joanna Hinton-Malivoire
Picture research by Mica Brancic
Production by Victoria Fitzgerald
Originated by Capstone Global Library Ltd
Printed and bound in China by South China Printing
   Company Ltd

14 13 12 11 10
10 9 8 7 6 5 4 3 2

**Library of Congress Cataloging-in-
Publication Data**
Spilsbury, Louise.
   Jellyfish / Louise Spilsbury.
      p.cm.—(A day in the life: sea animals)
   Includes bibliographical references and index.
   ISBN 978-1-4329-4000-3 (hc)
   ISBN 978-1-4329-4007-2 (pb)
   1. Jellyfishes. I. Title.
   QL377.S4S67 2011
   593.5'3—dc22
                                    2010000624

Acknowledgments

We would like to thank the following for permission to
reproduce photographs: FLPA p.19 (Minden Pictures/Ingo
Arndt); Getty Images pp.18, 23: polyp (Getty Images);
Image Quest Marine pp.12, 23: bell (V&W/Mark Conlin),
13 (Peter Parks), 17, 23: tentacle (Chris Parks), 21 (Andre
Seale), 22 (Kare Telnes); Photolibrary pp.4 (WaterFrame/
Underwater Images/Franco Banfi), 5, 23: swarm (Oxford
Scientific Films (OSF)/Howard Hall), 6 (imagebroker.
net/Ingo Schulz), 7 (age fotostock/Morales Morales), 8
(Index Stock Imagery/Wayne & Karen Brown), 9 (Corbis),
10, 23: zooplankton (Animals Animals/Tim Rock), 11,
23: venom (Oxford Scientific Films (OSF)/Paul Kay), 14
(WaterFrame - Underwater Images/Franco Banfi), 15
(Tsuneo Nakamura), 16, 20, 23: sense cells (Tips Italia/
Reinhard Dirscherl).

Cover photograph of jellyfish at Monterey Bay Aquarium
reproduced with permission of Corbis (© Atlantide
Phototravel/Stefano Amantini). Back cover photograph
of a swarm of moon jellyfish reproduced with permission
of Photolibrary (Oxford Scientific Films (OSF)/Howard
Hall). Back cover photograph of tentacles reproduced with
permission of Photolibrary (imagebroker.net/Ingo Schulz).

We would like to thank Michael Bright for his invaluable
help in the preparation of this book.

Every effort has been made to contact copyright holders
of material reproduced in this book. Any omissions will
be rectified in subsequent printings if notice is given to the
publisher.

All the Internet addresses (URLs) given in this book were
valid at the time of going to press. However, due to the
dynamic nature of the Internet, some addresses may have
changed, or sites may have changed or ceased to exist
since publication. While the author and publisher regret
any inconvenience this may cause readers, no responsibility
for any such changes can be accepted by either the author
or the publisher.

Contents

Some words are shown in bold, **like this**.
You can find them in the glossary on page 23.

What Is a Jellyfish?

A jellyfish is a soft-bodied sea animal.
Jellyfish live in oceans all over the world.

swarm

There are many different types of jellyfish.

Sometimes jellyfish live in groups called **swarms**.

What Do Jellyfish Look Like?

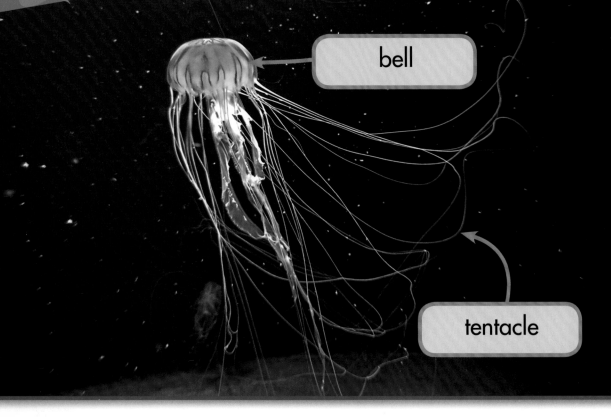

bell

tentacle

A jellyfish has a soft, round top called a **bell**.

Tentacles hang down from the bell.

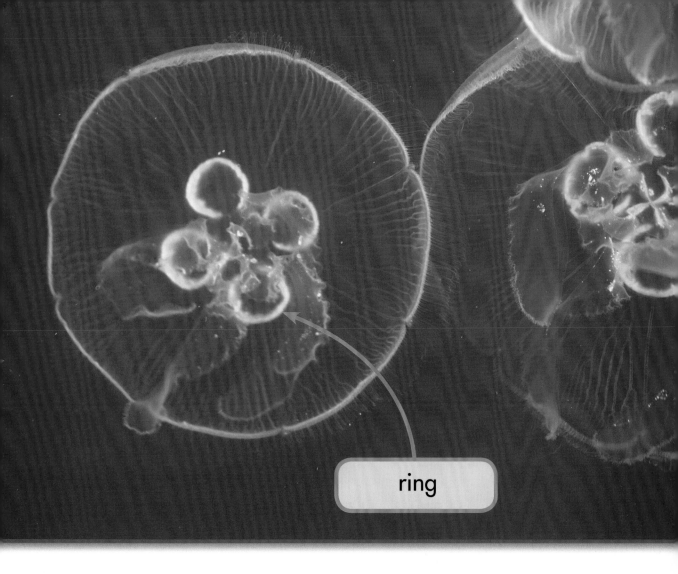

ring

The moon jellyfish has a pale blue or pink bell.

A moon jellyfish has four horseshoe-shaped rings at the top of its bell.

What Do Jellyfish Do?

Moon jellyfish stay in shallow waters near land.

They can find food near the top of the water.

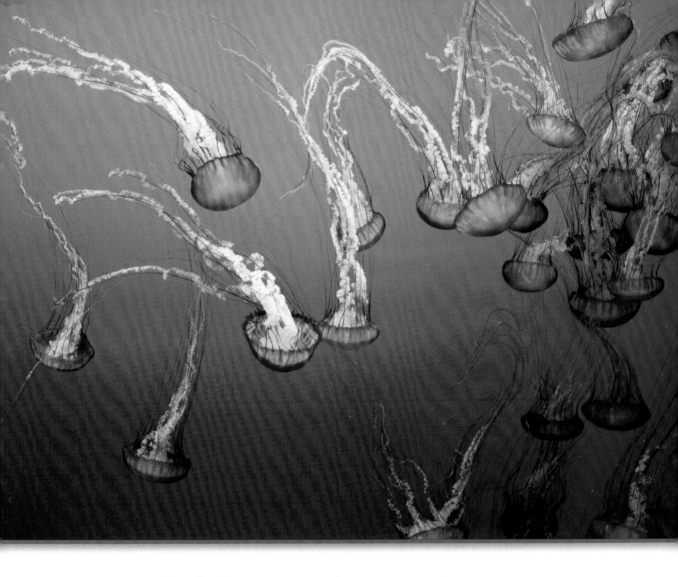

Some jellyfish move deep underwater in the day.

At night they return to the top to find food.

What Do Jellyfish Eat?

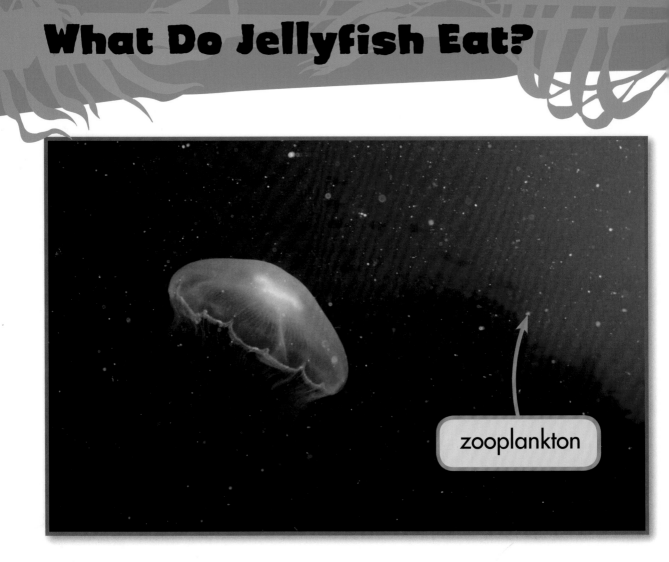

zooplankton

Moon jellyfish feed on tiny **zooplankton** that float in the water.

Zooplankton includes tiny shrimp-like animals and young crabs or lobsters.

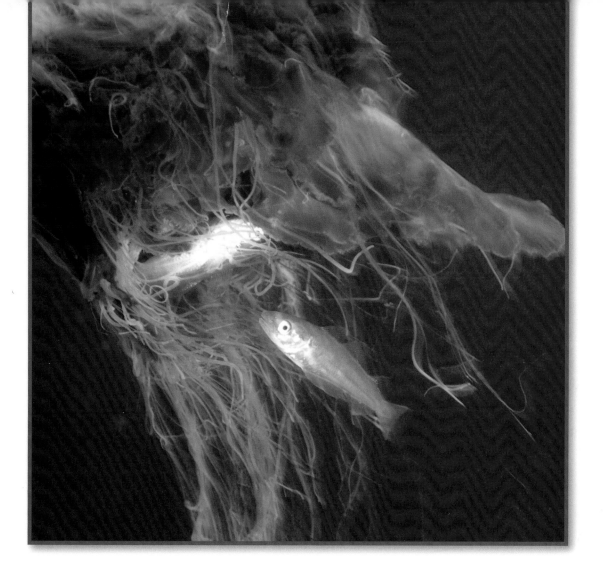

Larger jellyfish eat bigger sea animals, such as fish or shrimps.

Some jellyfish also eat other types of jellyfish!

How Do Jellyfish Catch Food?

tentacle

Jellyfish catch food with their **tentacles**.

Jellyfish have **venom** in their tentacles that stops animals from moving.

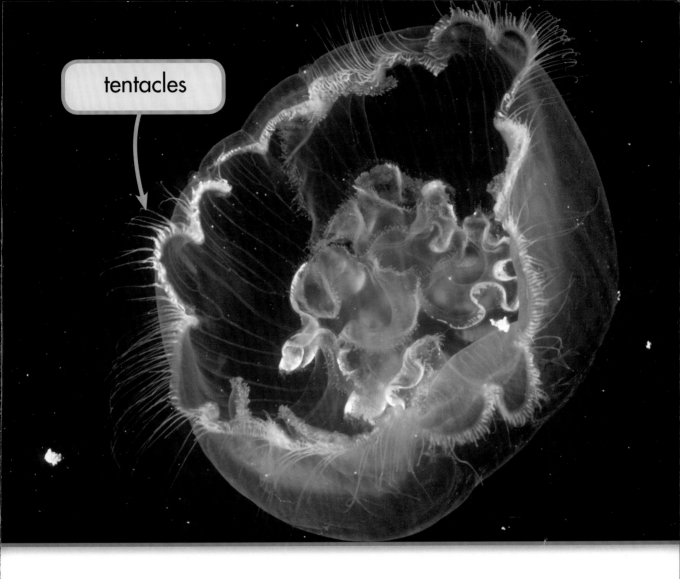

tentacles

Moon jellyfish trap food in the sticky slime on their tentacles.

Then the food is carried to the jellyfish's mouth.

How Do Jellyfish Move?

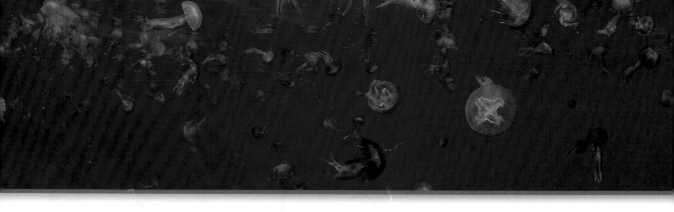

Jellyfish travel a long way floating in the water.

The ocean carries them along as it moves.

Jellyfish can move by opening their **bell** and filling it with water.

Then they squeeze their body tight and push out the water to make them move.

Do Jellyfish Have Senses?

Jellyfish do not have eyes or ears.

They use special **sense cells** to find their way.

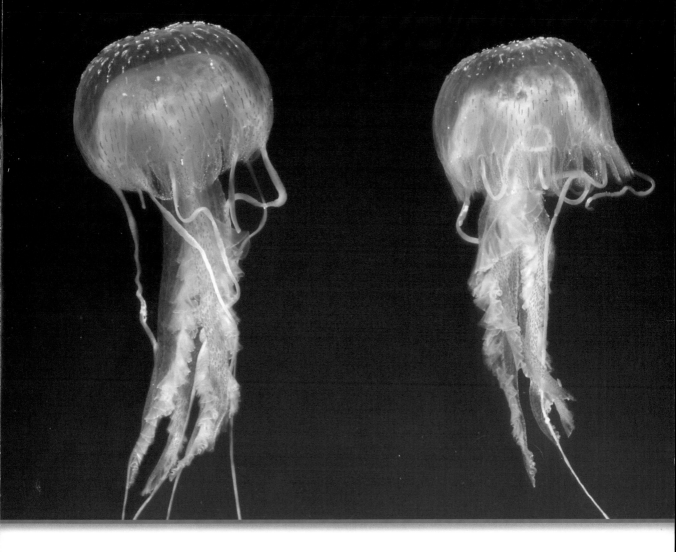

Some sense cells tell jellyfish to move toward or away from light.

Jellyfish have other sense cells to smell and taste and to balance in the water.

What Are Jellyfish Babies Like?

young jellyfish

Moon jellyfish eggs grow on the underside of a female's **bell**.

Young jellyfish hatch out of the eggs and stick onto rocks.

When the young jellyfish stick to rocks they are called **polyps**.

The polyps float away and some grow into adult jellyfish.

sea turtle

Some turtles, fish, and other jellyfish hunt jellyfish.

These animals do not feel the stings from jellyfish **tentacles**.

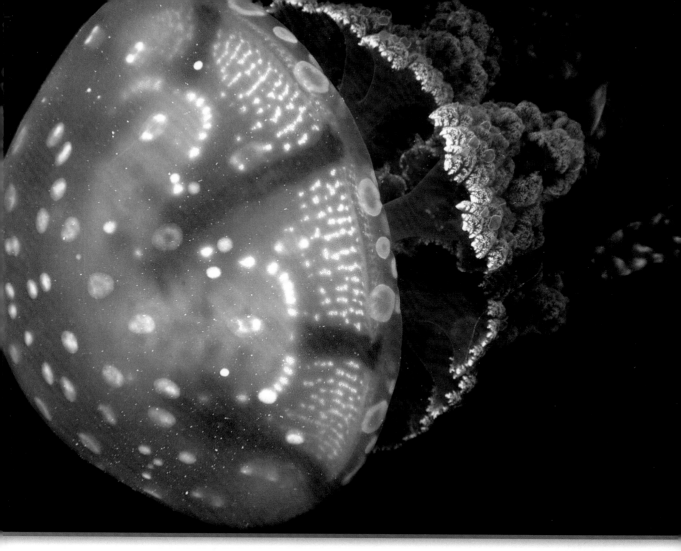

Some jellyfish start to glow if they are attacked at night!

Lights make the jellyfish look bigger to scare off its attacker.

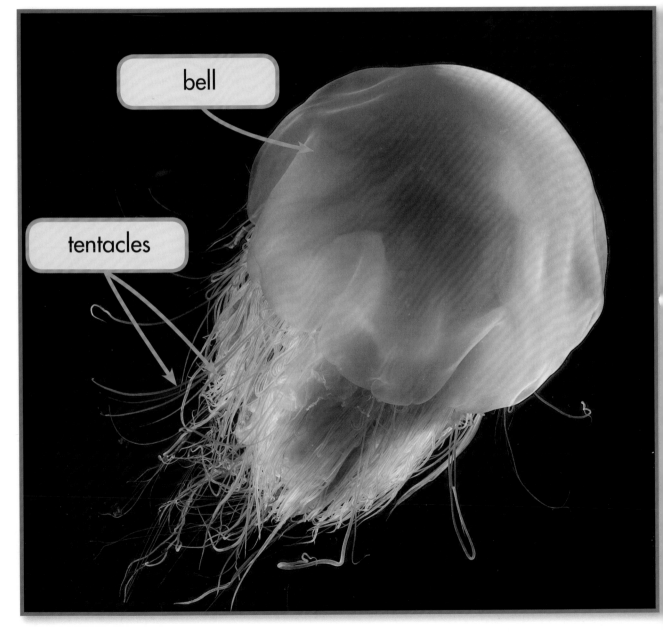

bell

tentacles

Glossary

 **bell** body of a jellyfish

 **polyp** early stage in the life of an animal such as a jellyfish

 **sense cells** parts of a jellyfish's body that can tell the animal about the world around it

 **swarm** group of jellyfish

 **tentacle** long, thin part of a jellyfish's body that it uses for feeling and catching food

 **venom** poisonous juice that can kill animals

 **zooplankton** tiny animals that float or drift in the sea

Find Out More

Books

Stone, Lynn M. *Jellyfish* (Marine Life). Vero Beach, Fl.: Rourke Publishing, 2006.

Wearing, Judy. *Jellyfish* (Wow World of Wonder). New York: Weigl Publishers, 2009.

Websites

Watch a video on jellyfish and find out all about them at: **kids. nationalgeographic.com/Animals/CreatureFeature/Jellyfish**

For photos and facts about box jellyfish go to: **www. sciencenewsforkids.org/articles/20050518/Note2.asp**

Index